I0027139

HEARTBEAT TO HAPPINESS

EIGHT

PRINCIPLES

OF LIVING A

HAPPY LIFE

SHELLY CADY

Heartbeat to Happiness

Eight Principles of Living a Happy Life

SHELLY CADY

Copyright© 2014 Shelly Cady

All rights reserved.

All rights reserved. No part of this publication may be reproduced, stored in a retrieval system, or transmitted in any form or by any means without the written permission of the publisher.

This publication is designed to provide information and motivation to its readers. It is distributed with the understanding that neither the publisher nor the author are engaged to render any type of psychological, legal, or any other kind of professional advice. The content of this book is the sole expression and opinion of its author. Neither the publisher nor the author shall be liable for any physical, psychological, emotional, financial, or commercial damages, including, but not limited to, special, incidental, consequential or other damages.

Printed in the United States of America

Dedication

THIS BOOK IS DEDICATED to my parents, Bill and Opal Cady, who taught and showed me what happiness was and is, without ever mentioning the word. Physically, I love and miss you both. Spiritually, I feel you both still with me every day.

Acknowledgements

I WOULD LIKE TO acknowledge the people who guided me in being able to share my story with the world: Greg S. Reid, for mentoring me; Stacey O'Byrne for coaching me; Derlene Reeves Hirtz for believing in me and being my sounding board; Bill and Opal Cady for instilling in me the principles that I share within this book.

Table of Contents

Foreword

"Happiness is found in doing, not merely possessing."
- Napoleon Hill

THOSE WHO HAVE MET ME know that I have adopted an attitude about life. To me, life is always good, whether I'm at work or play. When asked how I am, my standard reply is, "Always good." And I am.

I've spent years enjoying my work and mentoring others on their road to success. During that time, I have inevitably found that an individual's attitude will profoundly impact their success and happiness. A negative attitude will produce negative results, and a positive attitude will produce positive results. It's a principle that determines whether one approaches any endeavor with enthusiasm and gusto, or whether they give a half-hearted effort, seemingly giving up before they begin. An attitude is a tool that is available to everyone who wants to improve their lives, but too often, we overlook the impact that it can have on our success and happiness.

The greatest thought leaders of our time have passed on success principles and philosophies that support the fact that happiness is not a destination, but rather a journey. Our state of mind is an inside job, regardless of outside influences. When we are in control of our attitude and state of mind, we have the ability to hold negativity at bay and an even greater ability to see the opportunities and possibilities that await us each and every day.

I've found that the key to true success is doing what you love. I've often said, "If you do what you love and love what you do, you'll have success your whole life through." Not only will you be successful, but you'll also be immensely happy … or like me, "always good." When you enjoy what you do, work won't be a four-letter word. Instead, it will be something you *want* to do—something that you're excited about doing. As a result, you can't help but be richly rewarded with all of the things that make you happy!

Shelly Cady loves what she does, and she is committed to helping others live a happy and prosperous life. In this book, she shares the eight principles she has implemented throughout her life so her readers can experience the same satisfaction and fulfillment in both their personal and professional lives.

When I first met Shelly, I was impressed by her genuine enthusiasm and desire to help others. Her positive attitude about life and work is refreshing and one that she portrays in everything she does. An avid student of success, she has now become an enlightening teacher, one who will inspire and motivate you to become an active participant in the creation of the life you desire and have always wanted. The heartwarming stories and strategies she shares in *Heartbeat to Happiness* produce immediate results and remind each of us that life is a gift that should be celebrated, all day, every day.

Begin today to use the simple, but powerful, principles in this book to transform your life and the way you perceive it. Don't wait another day. Grab the life you want by the reins, let your heart beat to happiness, and enjoy every minute of the incredible ride!

Keep smilin'!

Greg Reid

Motivational Keynote Speaker and Bestselling Author, www.BookGreg.com

Introduction

"No one drifts to success."
- Napoleon Hill

NAPOLEON HILL NEVER MET ME, but he knew me well. For many years of my life, I was what Hill called a drifter. In his book, *Outwitting the Devil*, which was published after his death and annotated by Sharon Lechter, Napoleon Hill defines a drifter as an individual who lacks purpose, seemingly going from one day to the next without exerting any thought toward their life. A drifter has no plans—their mind (and, therefore, their life) floats along in no particular direction, taking them aimlessly from one place or job to the next, along a path that leads to nowhere.

When you float through life without a plan, you have absolutely no idea where you'll end up. Even worse, though, you'll fail to be aware of your journey and the experiences and opportunities that present themselves along the way. You could either drift through life or be more like me and find you aren't aware of your passion and purpose. Neither path will bring you fulfillment or happiness in life.

Since I've been out of school, I've had a few jobs and have done well at each. First, I had a non-traditional job in warehousing management. It paid well, and I was the first female to receive a promotion to supervisor. I advanced and did rather well, although it wasn't a career that brought me the fulfillment that only comes from knowing you're doing what you love and are meant to do.

Next came retail, which suited me at the time because I was able to start small without a large investment. Again, I liked the job and had success. But something was still missing—the drive that comes from knowing I was fulfilling my passion and purpose in life.

Suddenly, though, while we're drifting along, we realize that the years have passed without any of the joy, happiness, or fulfillment that comes from aligning ourselves with our true talents and ambitions. We've had experiences, sure, but we took them for granted as we floated from one to another. As a result of the lack of participation in our own lives, we miss out on the joy and rewards that the journey offers.

Napoleon Hill said that 85 percent of the people in this world are drifters and non-participants in their lives. They leave their lives to chance, with no control over their destination. I was one of them. It wasn't until I stopped following a random path that I became a part of the minority—when I did, I realized that it's the journey, not the destination that matters in life.

So many of us, me included, are racing through life trying to get to that final destination of total success and happiness. There are only two problems with that: one, it doesn't exist; it's only an illusion, and the second is that we spend no time appreciating the journey that we are on through life. We go through life on auto pilot, asleep, and see very little of what we actually pass by.

In this book, you'll learn about my journey, as well as the journey of others who can help you become involved in your journey and have control over your destination. Above all, though, you'll learn about the principles I've employed along my journey—principles that will make your unique journey rewarding, fulfilling, and most of all, happy.

The principles in this book evolve around one single concept: Being happy. What is life without happiness? Being happy is more than a mood or an emotion—it's an attitude that can be applied to every aspect of life. Life is happening at every stage of your journey; don't wait until you reach your ultimate destination to fully enjoy it. Don't wait for the perfect job, the perfect house, and oodles of money in the bank. Live it now, with joy and happiness. Be fully involved and experience everything life has to offer—right where you are, right now. Given the choice, wouldn't most of us prefer to be happy if at all possible?

Regardless of what my career is and where it takes me, I've found that there are keys to living a content and joy-filled life, and those keys are available to you, regardless of your age, education, or career. You don't have to be in your dream job to be happy — happiness is a state that comes from within. It does not come externally, from material possessions, careers, or other people. After all, you can have the job you've always wanted, money in the bank, and a partner who means the world to you and still be stressed, burned out, or feel like you're going through the motions every day. If that's the case, you're drifting through a life without milestones or rewards.

The keys in this book provide the missing pieces to the life you've always wanted ... and the life you deserve to start living today. Without them, it doesn't matter what you do, how much you make, or who you're with— those are things that can be beyond your control. What you can control is your state of mind, your attitude, and the investment you make in your happiness.

Don't wait until all the pieces fall into place to begin experiencing and enjoying life. Something is bound to change, and you'll find yourself putting off the life you always wanted while you're waiting. Every minute of every day is one that you can never get back.

Stop drifting along. Stop waiting for something to happen before you allow yourself to enjoy what you have. Today is a gift that's too precious to waste! You can make it and every day rewarding, fulfilling and chock full of happiness.

Life is precious and meant to be enjoyed; may your journey through it be a memorable one.

Shelly Cady

"You can live a whole life time never being awake."
— Dan Millman, *Way of the Peaceful Warrior*

Chapter One

Got Attitude?

"A positive mental attitude is the right mental attitude in all circumstances."
- Napoleon Hill

YOUR MENTAL OUTLOOK ON life will dictate the experiences you have. If you have a poor attitude, you'll perceive your life in a negative manner. If your attitude is indifferent, you're likely to feel that your life is uneventful, lacking any stimulation or joy. On the contrary, though, if you have a positive attitude, watch out! Your life will be brimming with positivity, happiness, and rewards, regardless of what comes your way.

Why do some people go through life happy and content, while others are seemingly content being miserable? It's not what happens or doesn't happen in their lives ... it's their attitude.

Attitude. We've all got one—sometimes, it can fluctuate, depending on our circumstances at the time. Still, we have an overall mental attitude that we carry throughout our lives, one that becomes a part of our personality as it influences the quality of our life. It's more than the way we present ourselves to the rest of the world—it's how we interpret the events and situations that present themselves to us.

In the past, the word "attitude" has been given a negative connotation. *She has an "attitude."* The statement is intended to convey a poor or bad attitude; however, an attitude can be anything from ho-hum to awesome! The attitude we carry is our shield; it either keeps negativity or unhappiness at bay or it traps it inside of us and won't let it out.

As we go through the motions in life, the predictability of our routines puts us comfortably on auto pilot, where we exist, but fail to appreciate life. Too many people hustle and bustle through their days, only to find that they have to start over again tomorrow. They don't live—they exist—sacrificing their passions, interests, desires, and happiness. On the other hand, there are others who, regardless of what does or does not happen in their lives, manage to find joy in every moment. Their positive mental attitude brings them happiness, even when circumstances don't appear to support it.

Attitude is non-tangible, but it certainly produces tangible results. Have you ever met someone who is calm, even in the face of impending danger? Or how about the person who is always positive and "up," regardless of what life brings their way? The difference between them and everyone else is their attitude, and it is that attitude that influences the way they view the world and their experiences throughout life.

I've witnessed firsthand the impact attitude has on our happiness. In the past, I was in the retail business, where I sold Life is Good® apparel. I quickly learned that people weren't buying a brand—they were buying an attitude. It was there that I was privileged to encounter and know people with amazing attitudes. My customers were from all walks of life, but it was their experiences that made them unique. Among the most memorable were those who were battling cancer or another serious illness. Because of their circumstances, nobody would have blamed them if they were discouraged or sad. However, that wasn't the attitude they chose to adopt. Nearly every one of them was determined to have a positive attitude as they enjoyed life, regardless of what they were going through at the time. Their attitude is what carried them through and kept them strong. They were happy to be alive, and every day was one to be thankful for! They purchased the apparel to reinforce and reflect their attitude.

Such positivity in a time of uncertainty is a source of inspiration we can all tap into when we become discouraged. It's proof of the power that our mental attitude has over our happiness and success in everything we do.

What is an attitude? Your attitude is the way you respond to things, good or bad. It's how you approach your responsibilities, view your life, and interact with the people you meet. And it's unique to you. Your attitude is the product of your past, your beliefs, and your opinions. It's also the one part of your personality that can be changed by simply hitting a switch in your mind.

What is your outlook when you get up in the morning? Do you say, "I have to go to work?" or do you say, "I get to go to work!" There is a difference, and that difference is immense. That difference is attitude, and it will influence the way you think, act, and feel all day long.

The first step to insuring a happy life is to have a positive attitude. A good attitude will see you through virtually every obstacle you might face on any given day. It's like a suit of armor that prevents anything from getting in and eating away at your happiness and contentment.

Does that mean you should look at everything as being only good? No, not at all. There are many people who have been the victims of natural disasters who don't believe it was a "good" thing. However, it is those who realize that they cannot change the past and choose not to dwell on it that are able to overcome the unexpected and make the best of it. They are the ones who are able to focus on what they do have, rather than on what they don't have or have lost. In other words, they are able to find something good in even the most trying situations.

A good attitude will affect your outlook and results in everything you do. It seeps into all aspects of your life. It affects every person you encounter and influences whether they want to approach or interact with you. Napoleon Hill once said, "Your mental attitude attracts to you everything that makes you what you are." Have you ever seen a sullen teenager, upset because they don't want to be where they are, doing what they're doing? They certainly aren't a people magnet, are they? On the other hand, have you ever met someone who radiated joy—so upbeat and happy that you found yourself drawn to them without knowing why? Their attitude attracted you to them. A positive attitude radiates to the people they meet and helps them to see their life from a positive perspective that naturally pulls people to them, instead of pushing them away.

No matter what is happening in my life, I've maintained a good attitude—every day. Maintaining a good attitude daily allows me to have a positive viewpoint or perspective on events that occur throughout my life. I've found it's not what we encounter in our life that matters, but how we look at it. I call this the "reverse peephole." The reverse peephole allows me to see what is on the opposite side of the door. Most of us go through life looking out the peephole, watching for what is coming at us next. We might be hoping for the best, but fearing the worst. At the very least, it's common to have some degree of anxiety from the unknown. But what makes something good or bad? Our attitude and our perspective.

One person can see the glass half empty, wishing they had more and feeling deprived. Another person, though, can see that same glass entirely differently — it's more than sufficient for what they need right now, and they're grateful for it! One person might see a career change as negative, even scary, while another can view that same career move as exciting and full of potential opportunities. Who is most likely to succeed in that new career? Of course, it's the person who looks forward to the adventure, not the person who is upset and scared. Again, the difference is all in the attitude.

What if we viewed everything that came at us as positive and good? I mean EVERYTHING. I'm a firm believer that everything that happens to us has some good or useful purpose. A great example is the person who wakes up late and misses their flight. Rather than only looking forward to what they expected to come next (catching their plane), they were upset. But when they looked on the other side of the door, they might have been thankful that they had time to relax, catch up on their work, or simply accept that there was nothing they could do about it now and make the best of their situation. Who is going to have a better day?

The way we feel and respond to everything in our life depends on our beginning attitude, what we focus on and believe in. Is your glass half empty or half full? It is a common expression, used rhetorically to indicate that a particular situation could be a cause for optimism (half full) or pessimism (half empty), or as a general litmus test to simply determine an individual's worldview. The purpose of the question is to demonstrate that virtually every situation may be seen in different ways, depending on one's point of view. Yes, there may be trouble, doubt, or fear in a situation, but that same situation can also present opportunity. When your attitude only lets you see the negative, you'll miss all of the potential that the positive has to offer. Even worse, a life of negativity is void of hope—a life without hope is a very empty one, indeed.

Our attitude is the way we express our perception of events, objects, and people. Perception is unique to every individual, and it is simply one's interpretation of reality. I like to think that I have a great attitude. It is what keeps me smiling ... always. There is something good or positive that can be gained from every event in life, if you choose to find it. If you view or perceive every event that occurs, every situation that you encounter, and every person that you meet as good and positive, it's impossible not to smile through life! A smile can be all it takes to change our attitude. In fact, something as small as a smile has the power to change our life.

1. Want to be More Attractive? Smile!

   Studies have proven that a smile can be the most attractive thing we can wear. So stop fretting about your clothing and your hair and focus on your smile! A study by the American Academy of Cosmetic Dentistry revealed that approximately 96 percent of American adults feel that a smile makes people more attractive. People want to be around people who are happy; we are naturally drawn to them. A smile is like a magnet that attracts people to us, letting them know we are friendly, open to interaction, approachable, and likeable.

2. Smiling Alters Your Mood

   Have you ever been in a bad mood and somebody started laughing—and before you knew it, you were laughing, too? You were upset and didn't want to smile and laugh, but when you did, you found you weren't so upset, after all. That's because smiling and laughing psychologically tricks your mind into feeling better. So the next time you're sad, depressed, or upset, flash your pearly whites and smile. It's a safe bet that you'll find your mood changes very quickly.

3. A Smile is Contagious

When you walk into a room and everyone is laughing and smiling, what do you do? Chances are you will smile—even if you don't know why. The same holds true if you walk into a room where everyone is sad—you'll adopt the same behavior, again without even knowing why. When you smile, not only do you change your mood, but you also have the power to change someone else's mood. It's a natural and spontaneous way to make everyone happier! So, go ahead and smile—you're likely to find yourself surrounded by other smiling people in no time at all.

4. A Smile is a Stress Reducer

Stress is internal, but it makes itself known externally. When you see someone whose lips are pursed, brows are furrowed, or who looks tired and spent, the odds are pretty good that they're suffering from some level of stress. Yes, you can actually see stress. If you find you're feeling stressed, stop everything and smile, even if you don't feel like it. A smile is an easy and free stress reducer, and as a bonus, it eliminates the "worry lines" that etch themselves into our faces.

5. Want to Improve Your Immune System? Try Smiling!

Studies show that people who smile often are less likely to get sick. Because smiling reduces stress and enhances relaxation, it also helps boost the immune system. So the next time you're trying to prevent a cold or flu, smile when you reach for the hand sanitizer.

6. A Smile Lowers Blood Pressure

This is not an old wives' tale. Studies have shown that smiling causes a reduction in blood pressure. Again, that is because smiling reduces stress and is a natural aid to relaxation. For this reason, it is also claimed that our hearts benefit from smiling and that smiling can add years to our life. As you can see, a smile is definitely one of the heartbeats to happiness.

7. A Smile Makes Us Look Younger

Not only can smiling help us live longer, but it can also make us look younger. It's a win-win! When we curve our muscles upward in a smile, it reverses the signs of aging, lifting what gravity has lowered. Suddenly, our little frown lines disappear and our face is lifted, making us look lighter and brighter. So if you want to erase five or ten years from your face and create a youthful glow that defies your years, opt for a smile, rather than a face lift.

8. The Physical Effects of Smiling Make You Feel Good

Not only does a smile have a strong effect on our mood, but it makes us physically feel better, as well. That's because every time we smile, our body releases endorphins, serotonin and natural pain killers. Combined, these make us feel better. Therefore, a smile is a drug-free pain killer that requires no supplements and has no side effects!

9. A Smile Represents Success

Really? Yes! People who smile are perceived to be more successful. They convey confidence in themselves, which others interpret as success. In business, a smile is a powerful tool that influences the way people respond to us. When we smile, we are viewed as open, approachable, and even a better candidate for promotions.

10. A Smile Influences Your Attitude

Do you want to be more positive? Do you want to get more joy, happiness, fulfillment, and contentment from life? Then smile! It's the greatest attitude adjustment you'll make! A smile makes us feel better, it alters our mood, and it reduces stress.

As a result, we can't help but be more positive! Go ahead, try to be sad, depressed, overwhelmed, or negative when you're smiling. I bet you can't!

Simply put, if you want to have a good attitude, just smile! It's not easy to be down when you're smiling. And it will help you see (and, therefore, live) your life from a new, better perspective—one where every day has a positive impact on your overall happiness and outlook.

What if it's not enough? What if you find that you're still plagued with worry, anxiety, stress, dissatisfaction, or you're drifting along with a lack of interest or enthusiasm? Well, in that case, I recommend that you try faking it. Fake it until you make it, and "act as if." Act as if you're wildly happy! Hum a little tune as you go about your day. Put a skip in your step as you walk into work. Share a sunny and joyous "Good Morning!" with your family and coworkers, even if you don't feel like it. Act as if you're happy, *especially* when you're not!

If you are constantly smiling, even if you feel differently on the inside, eventually the inside catches up with the outside. If on the outside you are smiling, laughing, and loving life, how can you avoid really feeling that way? Our brain is an amazing vehicle. If we convince it of something, i.e., *I am happy*, the brain will make that come true! That's because we are conditioned to respond inwardly according to our outside influences. By smiling and being positive, even if you're faking it, you're attitude will align itself with what it is being exposed to.

When it comes to the attitude you adopt, you always have a choice. You also have the power to change your attitude to create the results and experiences you want in life. When something happens and you catch yourself thinking negatively about it, stop yourself immediately and look for the good in it. There always is something good and positive in every situation. There is always something that we can gain by it. Remember, it is how we view things that determine if they are good or bad in our mind. Thankfully, we always have a choice on how we view anything in our life.

Perhaps the best example of how our viewpoint affects our attitude comes from Thomas Edison. When visited by Walter Mallory, a long-time associate, Edison explained that he had conducted more than 9,000 experiments in an effort to create a storage battery. Mallory sympathized with Edison for having invested so much work and time without achieving his desired results and asked, "Isn't it a shame that with the tremendous amount of work you have done, you haven't been able to get any results?" Edison surprised Mallory with his response. "Results! Why, I have gotten a lot of results! I now know several thousand things that won't work."

Edison could have been discouraged. He could have been frustrated or even given up. But Edison didn't choose to see his work as a failure—he chose a refreshingly positive perspective, believing that all of his attempts were bringing him one step closer to success. Each attempt was not a failure—it was a success in itself, through the process of elimination. It was his attitude—his *positive attitude*—that ultimately produced Edison's success in that invention and many others.

We have that choice of how we want to look at things and view them. If you have a good attitude from the onset, you are more likely to see the good in the event immediately. The beauty of a good attitude isn't only that it's yours, though—it's that you can share it with others. Yes, you have the power and the ability to influence the way other people act and respond.

I like to think of it as giving others a lift, an elevator ride, to the top floor of happiness with me. I can bring a smile to their face when they don't have one. I can brighten their day or their life by sharing my good attitude with them. It feels incredibly great to be able to brighten someone else's day or give something of myself to another. Each time I do, it only makes me feel better. It's the gift that reciprocates!

I can share my positive viewpoint with another and allow them to see a totally new perspective—one that they might have overlooked or never seen before.

It can be as small and effortless as a smile. Have you ever walked by someone who looked really down, then you smiled at them and they gave you a big smile back? That smile made you both feel better. Internally, most of us need to feel a connection with others. We need to know that we are a part of their lives and that we have a positive impact on the people we see. In short, it makes us feel good to make others feel good, even if it's just sharing a smile. If not for the long term, at the very least, it made them happy for a few minutes.

There are other benefits to having a good attitude. You see, it is our attitude that dictates our actions. A negative attitude is full of fear, doubt, anxiety, and/or stress. It refuses to let us make changes or explore opportunities. By removing a negative attitude, we open our world to the fact that we have choices.

If we don't like anything about our present situation, we can always change it. But if we have a poor attitude, we'll always look for reasons not to. In other words, we can only see the cons, never the pros. For instance, if you aren't happy in your career, a negative attitude will keep you there because you'll be looking for what could go wrong if you made a change. *It will take too long to get a degree; I'm too old to start over; they'll never hire me.* You get the idea. But why let a bad attitude hold yourself back from living the life you want?

As a child, you didn't have choices—you lived where you parents lived, in their house and in their town. You did what your parents wanted to do and maybe even chose a profession that met with their approval. As an adult, you now can do whatever *you* want. You are no longer tied to your parents' choices. The key, though, is to have a good attitude. By seeing the pros, the positives, you'll be able to make choices that can impact your happiness and success in life. You can choose to live in a different geographical area and do the things you really want to do. The choice is yours: either have a good attitude that allows you to make changes and create what you want, or have a poor attitude that makes excuses for why you cannot. The key is remembering that a positive attitude produces positive results. Henry Ford's infamous quote represents this well: "Whether you think you can or you think you can't, you're right."

The way you look at your life is crucial to the level of happiness you'll experience. The good news is that you can influence your attitude about your life and make it positive at any given moment. You don't have to be born with a winning attitude—it's a choice. It can be practiced and learned until it becomes second nature. It's a habit that's worth forming.

Starting today, you can influence the rest of your life simply by changing your attitude. Remember, your idea of a bad day might be someone else's idea of a good day. So look through the reverse peephole and see things from a different perspective. Keep your eyes open for the potential that lies on the other side of the door. Find the good in everything and everyone you encounter. And when you find you're feeling down, try a smile on for size. It's always a perfect fit, looks good on everyone, and is the best attitude adjustment you'll ever make!

Chapter Two

Be Upbeat, Be Optimistic

*"One optimist may wield more constructive influence
than a thousand pessimists."*
- Napoleon Hill

PEOPLE ARE OFTEN CATEGORIZED as optimists or
pessimists, but how many have honestly assessed
which category they fall into most of the time? To do
so, we must first explore what optimism really is. It's
much more than the person who always sees the glass
half full or who sees the world through rose-colored
glasses. Optimism is a mental attitude, and one that we
cannot hide from those in close proximity to us. It's
also a powerful influence on the outcomes of our lives,
as it determines how we act and react to different
circumstances and situations.

One of the most heartwarming stories about
optimism was actually told in a television commercial.
A young boy wanted to be a baseball player—not just
any baseball player, but the *best* player. In practicing,
he throws the ball into the air and as it drops down, he
takes a swing ... and misses. Strike one. Optimistic, he

says, "I'm the best hitter in the world." Then, he continues, once again throwing the ball up into the air, letting it fall and taking a swing. Strike two. Not one to be discouraged, he throws the ball into the air one more time, saying for the third time, "I am the best hitter in the world." He swings ... and misses. Strike three. Not missing a beat, he throws the ball into the air again, this time saying, "I am the best pitcher in the world." Optimism at its best.

Optimism is a mental attitude or view that interprets situations and events as being the best that they can be (optimized). This means that in some way, for factors that may not be fully comprehended, the present moment is in an optimum state. The concept is typically extended to include an attitude of hope that future conditions will be optimal, as well.

A broader sense of optimism is the understanding that all of nature, past, present and future, operates by laws of optimization. This understanding, although criticized by contrary views, such as pessimism, idealism, and realism, leads to a state of mind that believes everything is as it should be, both now and in the future.

As an optimist, I see all aspects of life as opportunity. I prefer to view life in a positive state and ready for the "picking" or achieving of my goals. I believe that anything that can be accomplished or conquered if we have the belief or desire to do so. As the cliché goes, if there is a will, there is a way. I know I'm not alone in that thinking; no goals are unachievable for an optimist. EVERYTHING that I may want to attain or achieve is possible; all I have to do is figure out a way to do so and move toward attainment of that goal or achievement.

How many times have you heard a friend or family member tell you that they can't do something? "I can't go back to school; I can't lose weight; I can't start my own business; I can't run a marathon; I can't ..." Then you ask them why, only to receive an answer that sounds bogus? They are not looking at the situation from an optimistic viewpoint. They haven't even given themselves a chance to succeed or fail. The only thing they have done is quit before trying.

A large part of being optimistic instead of a pessimistic is that we decide/choose how we want to look at things. We have that power—that control over our life and how we perceive the events that occur. As an example, let's presume that you lost your job. The pessimist looks at this situation and: blames others, feels sorry for themselves, sits at home and feels helpless because someone else has control over them, takes things out on their family, feels bad about themselves, and on and on ... The optimist looks at this same situation and says, "Wow ... guess there is something better out there for me!" They believe that there really is something better for them, and as a result, they actively look for a new and better position, accept the possibly that they weren't that happy in the position they lost, consider this to be an opportunity to learn a new trade or make an industry change, and they don't take the job loss as personal (unless they directly did something to force the loss). It's the same event for both the optimist and the pessimist, just two totally different perspectives on what occurred. Which one is most likely to have a positive, favorable outcome? In my opinion, it's the optimist.

It would be remiss to discuss optimism without addressing its counterpart, pessimism. We all know a pessimist—the chronic complainer who believes the world is against them. They are experts at complaining and finding the negative in any and every situation. Pessimists truly believe they cannot win for losing—in fact, they are adamant that they are destined to lose and that the universe will single them out and float a black cloud over their head everywhere they go. They operate their lives in such a way that they blame others or unknown forces for their plight and, therefore, see themselves as victims who are powerless over their circumstances. In addition, even if good things happen in their lives, and they do, they somehow manage to view it in a negative light.

The pessimist's woe-is-me attitude is in stark contrast to that of an optimist, who views nearly everything in a positive light. As a result, the optimist accepts what comes their way, finds the good in it, and then strives to find an opportunity in it. We hear stories of such optimists all of the time—even in the face of a setback, they prefer not to dwell on what happened, but to look forward and use their energies, thoughts, and actions to turn it into a positive. Walt Disney was told nobody would ever be interested in a cartoon mouse, but he never gave up. Donald Trump has had his share of financial problems, but he never let that stop him from becoming a financial powerhouse. The world is full of optimists ... they defy odds and walk after being paralyzed; they rise back from the bitter taste of defeat to enjoy the sweetness of victory; they inspire other optimists each and every day as they prove that circumstances don't control them; instead, they control their circumstances.

Helen Keller once said, "No pessimist ever discovered the secrets of the stars, or sailed to an uncharted land, or opened a new heaven to the human spirit." Born deaf and blind, she was also reported to be "dumb." However, her philosophy proves that she was, indeed, quite the opposite. Helen Keller struggled to learn so many things that we all take for granted. Against seemingly insurmountable odds, she became a spokesperson for those with disabilities, as well as a strategic thinker and motivator for everyone. Without a doubt, if anyone had justification to be a pessimist, it was Helen Keller. She could have accepted her limitations, and, therefore, the limitations they would impose on her life. But she didn't. Instead, she had a thirst for more and was driven to change her circumstances by taking action. Sure, she could never change the fact that she couldn't see or hear. But she could change her attitude toward her limitations and find a way to turn a seemingly negative circumstance into something positive in her life. In other words, Helen Keller saw that she was gifted with opportunity—opportunity to make a positive impact and influence on the lives of others.

I witnessed similar optimism in both the retail and insurance industries. People have accidents; they lose their belongings, vehicles, and homes. Yet, they rise above their circumstances and are grateful for what they do have, realizing they have their health, their families, etc. Some people who walked into my store to buy apparel were fighting illness; yet they were optimistic and despite, their circumstances, saw life as being truly good. Because they chose strength over weakness, positivity over negativity, and happiness over depression, that is what they brought into their life. As a result, regardless of what was happening in their life at the time, their life was happy!

Perhaps the greatest definition of a pessimist is that he or she always believes that something bad lurks in every corner and is sure to not only find them, but seek them out. They expect the worst possible results in everything they do. If that is the case, why even try? Pessimism is the world's worst motivator, while it is the best dream killer of all time. On the contrary, optimists always believe that something good lies ahead, even if they can't see it or don't know what it is. They are willing to try new things and explore possibilities because they haven't psychologically talked themselves out of it, convincing themselves that everything is a lost cause before even trying. And even if they don't get the results they want, they don't let that stop them from gaining from the experience.

Some call it faith—faith in the unknown. As an optimist I believe that things always work out as they are meant to. I believe that every success and failure has a purpose and there is something positive that I can take from everything that happens in my life. I can decide/choose how I view things, and things always occur as they should in the right time and manner. I know that I am at any given time right where I should be.

It is true that optimists are more successful than pessimists. First and foremost, they are willing to explore opportunities and possibilities because they haven't blocked out the potential for success. Optimists are more likely to be entrepreneurs and leaders—they are willing to take chances and risks and are known for their ability to influence others, a leadership trait that is invaluable. Knowing that, are all pessimists doomed to a life where fear, negativity, or acceptance keep them attached to the status quo? No, they are not. Just as we have the power and ability to change our attitude and perspective, we are also capable of changing our thoughts and beliefs.

Many believe that optimism is a trait we are born with—we cannot change who we are and how we think. They mistakenly think that, like our personality, being a pessimist or an optimist is ingrained into our psyche and we are powerless to change it. That can't be farther from the truth. People always have the ability to change their attitude and perspective.

How to Become Optimistic:

1. Choose an entirely different perspective.

Have you lost your job or had another "disaster" strike? Naturally, certain events can be viewed as negative. When they occur, purposely make a concerted effort to view the event in a more favorable light. Sure, it might have been a good job, but find the positives—you can find another job, you might find a job you like more, this is an opportunity to upgrade your skills, change industries, etc. Force yourself to see the pros and focus less on the cons.

2. Choose control over acceptance.

Bad things can happen, but they aren't the end of the world. When a pessimist loses a relationship or a career, they tend to accept that this is their lot in life. Instead, take control and take action—do something to improve your circumstances, life, finances, relationships, etc. If a relationship has ended, go out and meet new people. If you've lost a job, get back on the horse and into job-search mode. Those who take control move on much faster and have the greatest chance of success!

3. Surround yourself with positive people.

People who are negative and depressed will impact you and influence your thoughts. Like they say, misery loves company. But did you know that happiness is more likely to draw a crowd? If you have a tendency to be negative, surround yourself with positive people. You are the company you keep. They'll help you see things in a different light—and their positivity will rub off on you!

4. Learn what makes you feel good about life.

Find out what makes you feel good and put more of it in your life. What makes you feel lighter, puts a spring in your step? What puts a smile on your face and makes you happy? Whether it's the sunshine, flowers, music, puppies, or a hobby like painting, writing, or gardening, invite more of what makes you feel good and less of what doesn't into your world. When you experience more happy and fulfilling moments, you'll actually begin to believe that life is as good as it can possibly be!

5. **Bring something positive into every experience you have.**

Going on a job interview? Reward yourself for getting an interview, regardless of how it turns out. Turn your predestined thoughts of negative outcomes around by purposely bringing something positive and enjoyable into it. In that way, you can train your brain to stop thinking of everything in only a negative light and retrain it into believing that there is something good to be gained from all situations and events, regardless of the outcome.

6. **Keep a log of things that you are grateful for.**

It's difficult to be negative when you're grateful. Everybody that is breathing and living has something to be grateful for—reinforce it in your mind every day by making a point to write down something you are grateful for today. As a bonus, when you're grateful, the universe will actually go to work to bring you more of the very things you're grateful for!

7. **Do some soul searching.**

Sometimes, we have to dig deep and find out just why we think the way we do—maybe we adopted the way our parents thought or believed someone who once criticized us or told us that we "can't."

Find out where negative thoughts were introduced in your life, so you can address them, dismiss them, and replace them with positive thoughts that represent the person you are today.

8. Remember, it could be worse.

It can always be worse. Don't like your job? Think about a job that you'd like even less. Like the man who felt bad because he didn't have shoes until he met a man who didn't have feet, there is always something to be glad about. The next time you catch yourself dwelling on the fact that the glass is nearly half empty, turn your thoughts to the positive side and be glad that the glass is still half full.

Life isn't meant to be a bed of roses. After all, even roses have thorns. But if we focus entirely on the thorns, we'll never enjoy the beauty of the rose and the joy it can bring into our life. To live life at its fullest, we need to experience both happiness and sadness, good and bad, and success and failure. When we allow ourselves to experience the negative without letting it control us, we gives ourselves permission to enjoy the positive even more. We can then glean the opportunities that present themselves in those moments and benefit from them.

"A pessimist sees the difficulty in every opportunity; an optimist sees the opportunity in every difficulty."
-Winston Churchill

Chapter Three

Happiness is Being Yourself

"Hold a picture of yourself long and steadily enough in your mind's eye, and you will be drawn toward it."
— Napoleon Hill

WE ARE ALL IMPRESSIONABLE. As we are exposed to other people, whether in person, or through television, magazines, and the Internet, we are given access into the lives of people who will impress us. It's natural that we admire them and want to be like them. Advertising plays a major role in our influences, and it has successfully conditioned us to want to be more like others than ourselves.

I am a strong supporter, though, of being yourself. While we can certainly admire others and be inspired by them, we can do so without changing those things that are special and unique to us. It is in that uniqueness that our beauty lies. It is our uniqueness that holds our talents and passions, the inherent traits that are key to our success and happiness. They say no two people are alike. That's a very good thing! Can you imagine a world where we are all made from the same mold, where people think, look, and act alike? How boring we would be! Oh, how limited our lives would be if we were cookie cutter versions of each other.

To be yourself, sometimes referred to as being true to yourself, means to act in accordance with who you are and what you believe in. If you know and love yourself, you will find it effortless to be yourself. Just as you cannot love anyone else until you love yourself, you cannot be true to anyone else until you are true to yourself. If you aren't true to yourself and your unique qualities, you will only be dimming the qualities that were meant to shine.

Be who you are! Have the courage to accept yourself as you really are, not as someone else thinks you should be. Above all, have the courage to stand up for your convictions, despite pressure from others. Do not take action or pretend to be someone else for the sake of gaining acceptance. Many young people believe that when they do things to please their peers, such as drink when they shouldn't or behave and party in inappropriate ways, they will be popular and liked. When they succumb to peer pressure, they often go against the advice of their parents or their own common sense, only to find themselves in trouble and not accomplishing what they set out to do. In essence, they pulled themselves off their own path—the path to their unique destiny and success—and have chosen to blindly follow someone else's path. The problem is, though, that no one can ever be truly happy and fulfilled when they try to be or act like someone else or when they're tagging onto someone else's life.

When you do things that are not genuine or a reflection of the real you, you will become confused. You'll be confused because you won't know what makes you happy or what you want in life. This confusion makes it difficult to do just about anything, because you will not know whom to please, or how to please them. Above all, you won't be pleasing yourself—the real you that holds the key to your happiness.

Being true to yourself is a sign of respect for your talents, ambitions, and unique qualities. Self-respect comes from being true to who you really are and acting in accordance with your fundamental nature. When you respect yourself, others will respect you. They will sense that you are strong and capable of standing up for yourself and your beliefs. They will also trust that the person you represent yourself to be is authentic and real. That doesn't mean that the opinions of others should persuade or guide you. Not at all. You can respect the opinions of others without conforming to stereotypes or their expectations of you.

I am a firm believer that everyone should surround themselves with people they admire—people who inspire and motivate them. While it's easy to be inspired to like others, you should not be inspired to *be like* others. Instead, you should be inspired to be the best you that you can possibly be. Make the best of your physical appearance, your talents, your passions, and the gifts you bring to relationships and careers. Never jump on anyone else's bandwagon, trying to look like them, act like them, or live the life that they lead. If you do, you will never be happy. Even worse, you will rob the rest of the world from knowing you and benefitting from your individuality and the contributions only you can bring to the world.

We all have a need to belong and be accepted. This is especially true when we are children or teens. Those fundamental years compel us to fit in, rather than stand out. That's why they tend to follow the crowd. It's also the reason they cut school, smoke, drink, or take drugs in order to be accepted. Unfortunately, too many lack the self-love and confidence to resist peer pressure, which can be very strong.

Pressure to conform can come from both friends and family. When we are young, we are pressured to conform to our parents' expectations. Often, this is for our safety and well being; but sometimes, those expectations don't align with our dreams and wishes. For example, let's say your father is an attorney and, all of your life, he has only wanted you to follow in his footsteps. However, you are pulled in a different direction—you are creative and love the outdoors. You can't envision a life spent in a stuffy office in a job that you find boring and uninteresting. In this case, if you follow your own dream, you're likely to upset your father. However, if you don't follow your dream, unhappiness will set in as your talents and gifts are denied and you don't live a life that is true to your passions and uniqueness.

To be true to yourself takes courage. It takes courage to stand up for your convictions, ideals, and the values you hold dear. It takes courage to stand out from the crowd and follow your intuition and instinct. In order to know what that intuition is, you must be introspective, sincere, open-minded, and fair, especially to yourself. It does not mean that you are inconsiderate or disrespectful of others. Quite the contrary—you can always consider other people's feelings, advice, or ideas, but they should never be the sole reasons for any of your actions or decisions. Being yourself means that you will not let others define you or make decisions that you should make for yourself. Ultimately, the only person you have to answer to is yourself—you are responsible for your actions and your happiness.

In order to experience life at the fullest, you must have the conviction to live *your* life in the way that resonates with *you*—not someone else. Embrace your individuality—whether it's your appearance, your talents, your passions, your values, or your dreams. They are unique to you. Even identical twins raised by the same parents are different, often vastly so. They cannot escape their differences, nor should they try.

47

Imagine trying to live a life attempting to fit into someone else's mold!

Be true to the very best that is in you and live your life consistent with *your* highest values and aspirations. Those who are most successful in life have dared to creatively express themselves and, in turn, broaden the experiences and perspectives of everyone else. I have always felt that I must be true to myself, and by doing so, I must only be myself. For years, I was a drifter, not knowing what I really wanted or what my talents and passions truly were. I lived my life, but something was missing. That something was the devotion to my uniqueness and benefitting from knowing what fulfilled my passions and purpose. Eventually, I found those things, and when I did, I also discovered the key to my happiness.

When I was a drifter, I wasn't unhappy, but I wasn't aligned on the path I was meant to follow. Drifting didn't stop me from finding the right course, but it did delay the process. Don't get me wrong—I wasn't on the wrong path—I've always tried to stay true to myself. But at the time, I wasn't fully aware of what that was. It's a growing process that we all have to endure, and it can only come from self-discovery and knowing yourself.

I cannot be someone that I am not or someone that others want me to be. I also cannot pretend to be someone different than I am or someone that others expect me to be. That way of being has never fit for me. It has sometimes brought me pain when I did not fit in or when I was not the person that someone else wanted me to be or become. But, ultimately, that pain was much less than the pain I would have experienced by lying to others by showing up as someone that I was not.

As benefit, always being myself has won the trust of others. From their experience with me, they knew what to expect of me. There was never a question of who I was or how I might act or respond because I was always consistently me. Another wonderful attribute that comes from always being myself and remaining true to my values and convictions is that I have always known that the people who like me really like me for who I genuinely am. They don't like me for who I pretend to be or who I act like I am, just me! It's a great feeling to know deep in your heart that people like you just the way you are, without reservation or condition.

Being who I truly am allows me to live a life without regrets. I have no regrets for saying or doing something that is in disagreement with the person I am and the values I hold dear. Too often, when we act in a way that is inconsistent with our true selves, it spurs regrets, either for our actions or the way they affected us or the people we care about. I've learned that we cannot change the past; however, we always have control over the present. Because I am in tune with who I am and what is important to me, I will not regret tomorrow what I do or say today. I know that tomorrow I will still be comfortable in my own skin.

So many people spend years of their life without knowing true happiness. Usually, it's because they don't know themselves or are living a life that is incongruent with who they are. It's like they are a puzzle, but some of the pieces are missing. They cannot be complete until the entire puzzle is in place because there are aspects of their personality, their soul, and their purpose that are hidden from themselves and the world. Even hiding one little piece can leave them feeling less than whole.

One of the problems is that we all seek approval from others. We want to know that they like us, so we are careful not to offend anyone or take sides. We can be afraid to voice our true feelings for fear that others won't agree. Being non-committal in this manner prevents us from being true to ourselves and the things that matter most to us. It's called playing it safe — going with the flow or remaining on the sidelines — which is often what a drifter will do. In many ways, it's like being a spectator instead of a participant in life.

Everybody has something unique about them, and that uniqueness should be celebrated, not hidden. The beauty is that is that it is easier to be ourselves than it is to try to be something or someone we are not. It's like trying to put a square peg in a round hole. When you do, you will never fit. I liken this to a choir, one where everyone tries to sing the melody. But not everyone can sing the melody well. A rich baritone cannot sing a melody, and if he tried, nobody would be blessed with the unique qualities of his voice. We cannot all "fit in" and be alike; there must be harmony, too, and when there is, it creates the most beautiful music.

Being true to myself has allowed me to live a life of congruency—a life of agreement, harmony, and conformity. It allows me to have a healthy self-esteem and keeps me consistent to my own values. It also gives me a sense of peace, knowing that I am never in conflict with myself, for being in conflict with one's true self will be a source of inner turmoil and discourse.

Tips on Being True to Yourself

- Be who you are, be your genuine self
- Follow your own value system and common sense
- Listen to the advice of others, but make up your *own* mind
- Recognize, appreciate, and develop your unique talents
- Stand up for what you believe in and you will gain respect
- Know that being 'different' is a gift
- Understand that you are enriching others by being yourself

These are simple tips, but in order to carry them out, you must know yourself and listen to your conscience. If you're unsure of who you really are, listen to your heart. It beats to only one drummer—you!

"Always be a first rate version of yourself and not a second rate version of someone else."
— Judy Garland

Chapter Four

The Right Thing: It's the Right Thing to Do

"Real integrity is doing the right thing, knowing that nobody's going to know whether you did it or not."
- Oprah Winfrey

AT SOME POINT IN life, we're all called upon to do the right thing. Sometimes the right thing is clear and evident and requires no thinking. We just know what it is and do it without reservation. But there are other times when the right thing presents a dilemma — should we or shouldn't we ... nobody will ever know ... what if it comes back to bite me? These are issues we might ponder when contemplating if we should do the right thing ... or not.

Life gives us choices. We get to choose where we live and work, how we spend our spare time and who we spend it with. We get to choose the actions we take and the morals and values that we represent to the rest of the world. Doing the right thing also involves choice, ethics, morals, honesty and integrity. It is one of the biggest choices we'll ever make.

Choice is a powerful thing. Thus far, my perspectives on life have all involved choice. I have a choice to have a good attitude, to be optimistic, and to be true to myself. I also have the choice to do the right thing. I choose to do the right thing, even when nobody knows about it but me.

Imagine waiting for your ship to come in and, lo and behold, another ship comes in—it's not your ship, but it's got treasures that can be yours for the taking. Would you take them? These things happen to us all of the time, but on a much smaller scale. We find a billfold, or watch someone pull a few dollars out of their pocket, one of which drops to the floor. We walk through a parking lot and spot an iPhone next to a car door, or we enter a public restroom, where an engagement ring was inadvertently left on the edge of the sink. We witness an individual being bullied or another individual commit a crime. What would you do if any of these things happened? Would you step in and speak up? Would you see an opportunity to gain a few dollars or a valuable possession, especially if nobody knew that you were doing so? Or would you do the right thing by turning in the lost goods or trying to find the owner? The choice is yours, and it's an important one to make.

While there are those who think someone is so careless deserves to lose their money or possessions, there is usually much more to the story. The ten dollar bill that fell to the floor might have been all the money that person had to spend for food for the rest of the week. It could have been their bus fare to get home or to work. It might have been the last few dollars they were saving to purchase medicine for their child. Doing the right thing means taking a moment to realize you have a choice and reasoning that, although you could pick up that money and pocket it, you should pick it up and return it. After all, finding it doesn't make it yours.

Given these circumstances, I will always look for the rightful owner, whether they've lost money, a purse, a ring, or a pet. Just because I found something, that doesn't make it mine. The only thing that is mine is the choice of whether or not to do the right thing.

That choice exists even when you aren't the person who "finds" something lost. Sometimes, we have to be the eyes, ears, and voice for others who are wronged. The following story truly depicts this moral value, and it's one that's heartwarming and supports this life principle.

Only 19 years old, Joey Prusak was the manager of a Minnesota Dairy Queen restaurant. A blind man entered the restaurant, ordered food, paid for it, and turned to walk away from the counter. He didn't notice, though, that he had dropped a $20 bill during the process of pulling his money out of his pocket. However, a woman standing behind him did. Without a word, she reached down, picked up the $20, and dropped it into her purse. Joey Prusak witnessed her doing so, and so did other patrons in the establishment.

It wasn't Joey's money. He could have kept his mouth shut and not said a word, but he knew that wasn't the right thing to do. The right thing would have been for the woman to tell the gentleman he had dropped his money and return it to him. But she didn't. So Joey Prusak stepped in. He walked up to the woman and told her to return the money. She refused, adamantly stating that it was her money.

Appalled, Prusak repeated his request—return the money to the blind man or leave the restaurant. When she refused his request, he followed through, telling her he would not serve her and asking her to leave. She left $20 richer than she was when she walked in.

Joey Prusak did the right thing. He made the right choice, but then he surprised everyone by making another, even more noble, choice. Prusak walked to the table where the blind man was sitting and told him that on behalf of Dairy Queen, he'd like to give the man the money he had dropped. Pulling a $20 bill out of his own pocket, his gesture righted one woman's wrong.

This young man didn't do the right thing for fame or praise. In fact, it was another patron who witnessed the events unfolding who wrote and informed Dairy Queen's senior management about the event. The email was printed and placed on a wall, where it eventually captured attention on the Internet and went viral.

Joey Prusak could be you or me. We all have occasions where we are faced with whether or not we should do the right thing—whether we should speak up for others less fortunate or in need ... whether we should right someone else's wrong ... or whether we should stand idly by and let someone else become a victim simply because it's not any of our business.

My rule of thumb is to ALWAYS treat others as you want to be treated. How good would it make you feel if someone told you that you'd dropped some cash and handed it back to you? How good would it make you feel to know that someone, even a stranger, would speak up for you when it was the right thing to do? How much better would you feel when you pull that money out of your pocket and use it to pay your bus fare or buy your next meal?

The world needs more Joey Prusaks. If we want people to treat us kindly, we need to treat them with kindness, as well. If we want people to be just and fair, we must also be just and fair in our actions. This principle expands far beyond finding lost money or items. It's just as applicable to the way we treat people and the way we greet them. It involves living up to our word, our responsibilities, and our obligations.

Doing the right thing also means honoring your word. Be someone others can count on. If you tell someone you will do something, do it. When you borrow money, whether it's $10 from a friend or

$10,000 for a car, pay it back when you are expected to do so.

Doing the right thing is also a moral obligation. If you see someone who is in need, help them. That could mean speaking up for those who are bullied or victims, reporting information that could help prevent or solve a crime, or helping a person who is injured or ill.

The opportunities to do the right thing don't have to be monumental. In fact, most of the time, they are small things that don't take much time or effort. However, even the smallest of things can have a big impact. The way you treat others and the principles you live your life by will influence others; but most of all, they will influence you. When you do the right thing, you will attract others who are like yourself. It's the law of attraction, and the universe always brings you more of what you reflect. So, by doing the right thing, you're actually doing your part to make sure others do, too!

Most of the time when you do the right thing, there is no reward. There is no reward for returning the jacket you borrowed; there's usually no reward for paying the bank back on time. Joey Prusak didn't get a reward for helping out a valued customer. We don't need rewards for these things—the greatest reward is internal. Knowing that we did the right thing puts our conscience at ease and gives us the satisfaction of knowing that we made a positive difference in the lives of others. Another reward comes from knowing that others respect and trust us, regardless. It's about being true to our values, ethics, and morals. When we do the right thing, we feel good about ourselves, our lives, and how we treat others. In other words, we build character.

Napoleon Hill bases many of his success lessons on character. It is our character that defines us, and it also guides us to make the right decisions or to do the right thing. A person of good character is one who is reputable, in business and in life. It is someone who others respect, admire, and want to associate with on both a personal and professional level. Above all, it is the person who has good character who can hold their head up high, knowing that regardless of the outcome of their endeavors or efforts, they did the right thing. In the end, that's what matters most. Because, truth be told, if we cannot respect ourselves at the end of the day, it doesn't matter whether others do or not.

How do you know if you exemplify good character? Just look for the following traits; if you implement these in everything you do, you have the foundation of good, strong character.

The Josephson Institute, Center for Youth Ethics, has established six pillars of good character in their initiative entitled "Character Counts." Those pillars are Trustworthiness, Respect, Responsibility, Fairness, Caring, and Citizenship.

Trustworthiness

Trustworthiness is to be a person deserving of another's trust. It involves being honest at all times, even when honesty could create a problem or conflict in your own life. This includes being honest with your parents, teachers, employers, friends, family, and spouse. It's said that money tests honesty; when we come across money that isn't ours, it can be fairly easy to keep it, especially if no one else knows about it. Trustworthiness, though, means being honest with our conscience, which always knows right from wrong and honesty from dishonesty.

On a similar note, trustworthiness also steers clear of deception, cheating, and stealing, none of which are honest actions. Examples include cheating on a test, lying on a job application or resume, or taking something which is not yours to take.

Reliability is yet another aspect of trustworthiness. When people are trustworthy, others are assured they will be dependable. They will do what they say, be on time, complete tasks, and act in such a way that others know they can always be trusted, in virtually any situation or circumstance.

Trustworthiness is also about loyalty. In life, we are often asked to take a position. Others should know that we are loyal to those deserving, especially our family and friends who count on us to stand by them.

Respect

It's called the Golden Rule, and most of us learned it when we were young children. Do unto others as you would have them do unto you. In other words, treat others in the way you would like to be treated. Paramount to that teaching, it's important to treat others with respect, even (and especially) when we don't agree with them. It's about being tolerant of others and accepting that they have different beliefs without criticizing them or placing judgment on them because they don't agree with our philosophies or opinions.

Respect can be seen in the way we treat others, as well as the way we talk to and treat them. Having good manners is a sign of respect. Being aware of the language we use is another sign of respect. It's all about considering another person's feelings before we act or speak. One who is respectful never talks down to another or treats them rudely. They don't scream, threaten, or insult others and are able to act in a mature manner, recognizing that everyone can disagree and have differences without being angry or having a heated argument.

Responsibility

The third pillar of character is responsibility. Like dependability, it means that you should do what you are supposed to do. People need to be able to count on us to follow through and carry out our tasks and responsibilities when we say we will. Sometimes getting things done on time and in the right way requires planning. Sometimes it requires perseverance. In other words, we shouldn't quit when the going gets tough, when we lose interest, or when something better comes along. Responsibility is a trait that is taught to young children in group sports. When you become a member of a team, the team counts on every member! Children who sign up for youth sports or teams are often told they have to stick it out—quitting wouldn't be fair to the rest of the team.

Being responsible also means that you act in a mature manner—one that doesn't place yourself or others in harm's way. Drive responsibly, act responsibly, and think responsibly. To do that, one often finds themselves considering the consequences of their action or words. How will they affect you? How might they impact others? When you are responsible, you know you are accountable for what you say and do; therefore, you think before you act. It's an unselfish trait that keeps a lot of people out of trouble!

Fairness

Fairness is the next pillar, and again, it's another one that we learned early in our lives. When we were children, our parents and teachers taught us to play fair. Playing fair means playing by the rules, waiting patiently, taking turns, sharing, and abiding by the same set of guidelines that are expected of everyone else.

Fairness is also a philosophy. It's about making sure that we listen carefully and keep an open mind. It's a trait that jurors are requested to exemplify when they consider the facts of a case, without bias or prejudice, as they listen to and give all of the testimony due consideration and deliberation. The act of being fair means to treat all people alike, without displaying favoritism to any.

I'm sure there have been times when we've all rushed to judgment or blamed others for something without knowing all of the facts. Ultimately, these actions can lead us to a fair share of deserved embarrassment. When we implement fairness in our relationships, opinions, and actions, not only do we ensure that we aren't putting others in an uncomfortable or unfair position, we are also sparing ourselves of humiliation and the need to apologize for our mistakes.

Caring

The fifth pillar of character is caring. This pillar is one of my favorites. I am a people person. I'm drawn to people and intuitively want to help them. Caring represents the moral and ethical value which attracts me, and it has been a consistent value in all of my careers.

Caring doesn't mean you have to be a warm and fuzzy, touchy feely kind of person. It does mean, though, that other people are important and you're willing to express care and consideration for them as you interact with them. This could mean a measure as small as a kind greeting and a smile or a simple act of kindness. It involves being considerate and using manners. Caring also means that you say please and thank you, letting others know through your words, deeds and actions that you are grateful to them.

Compassion is one aspect of caring, and it's an important one that should be a part of all relationships. Through compassion, you let others know that you care. What good is caring about someone if you keep it hidden to yourself and don't let them know? Some people find it difficult to express compassion, saying that they're just not comfortable expressing themselves and their feelings. While it's always recommended that we should let people know we care about them when we do, compassion can be shown in others ways— opening a door, lending a hand, listening with your undivided attention, and asking someone how their day is or if they need your help. It could be a simple phone call or an email to check in with someone and let them know that you were thinking of them.

Caring can most certainly extend beyond people you know. When I sold Life is Good® apparel, I met many people every day—though they were strangers, I was privileged to hear their stories and be touched by them. From people who were facing serious illness to those who were struggling with other challenges, I couldn't help but care about them and admire their attitude and resolve. Without knowing them, I wanted to help them, even if it meant making their day a little brighter by being kind and compassionate. Being there for them, even in the smallest of ways, was, indeed, one of the heartbeats to my happiness.

Caring goes beyond the people we know and see every day. It means caring about issues and causes, showing compassion for a lost or injured animal, feeling for a sad child or a family who is down on their luck. It involves much more than being sympathetic, for sympathy is only a feeling. Instead, I am empathic—empathy is feeling that takes action. It doesn't take a great deal of action to let others know I care. It can be a small gesture, a kind word, a listening ear, a helping hand, or a passing smile. When we care about others, we let them know how we feel. When we express empathy, we show them how we feel.

Citizenship

The last pillar of character is citizenship. It's about knowing our role in the greater good of society, whether that is at school, at work, in the community, in organizations, or the government. In this sense, citizenship is not an allegiance to a nation—it's the acknowledgement that we are all obligated to do our part to make the world a better place. We cannot stand by idly and expect others to make the world just and good.

If you care about your neighborhood, get involved and know your neighbors. Be active as you work together to look out for each other and make a positive difference in your neighborhood. The same is true for school—do your share, whether it means volunteering, abiding by rules, keeping order, or cleaning up after yourself. Support your classmates and respect your teachers.

You can take citizenship up to the next level by getting involved in your community. Attend meetings and volunteer in local community affairs. Obey the law and adhere to the rules and regulations imposed by officials. Respect those in authority, whether they are police or emergency personnel, an alderman, or a mayor. Run for public office—become a member of the county board, offer your services on election day, make phone calls about issues that are important to you and others, serve on your school district's board of directors, become a volunteer firefighter, donate blood to the American Red Cross. There are so many things you can do and ways to offer your services that will have a positive effect on your community and its citizens.

Citizenship is also about being responsible for the environment. We are all impacted by pollution and litter, and we are all, therefore, charged with the responsibility of protecting the environment for ourselves and future generations. Simple acts, such as disposing of trash properly and recycling, can go a long way. They help us set an example for others that we have respect for the environment and are willing to take responsibility for its upkeep and beauty.

These six pillars of character all have one thing in common—they are all about doing the right thing. They represent a philosophy of thinking that accepts accountability and responsibility for our lives and the impact and influence we have on others. These principles don't cost us anything to implement; however, when we do, these six pillars will reward us with benefits that are far more valuable than money. Among them are pride, respect, dignity, and a clear conscience.

Life is a journey—and it's not the ultimate results we receive from our travels that hold the most value. It's the little things we do, day in and day out, that propel us toward happiness. When we do the right thing, no matter how large or how small, we are building the type of character that impacts not only the people we meet, but also the quality of our own life. Live life in such a way that you know you did the right thing and can hold your head up high—life doesn't get much better than that!

"Character is doing the right thing when nobody's looking. There are too many people who think that the only thing that's right is to get by, and the only thing that's wrong is to get caught."
- J. C. Watts

Chapter Five

Let Faith be Your Partner

"Faith is taking the first step, even when you don't see the whole staircase."

- Dr. Martin Luther King

YOU CAN'T SEE IT, but that doesn't mean it doesn't exist. Faith is intangible, meaning it cannot be touched; however, it can be felt. Although invisible, faith has the power to guide us through life's most trying times. Its presence in our lives can provide us with strength, endurance, and the reassurance that things will work out for the best. It is faith that gives people the belief that all things in life have a meaning and a purpose.

By definition, faith is confidence or trust in a person, thing, deity, or in the doctrines or teachings of a religion or view. To me, it is the belief in someone or something greater than me. It allows me to believe in a bigger picture or purpose than the one I can readily see.

A world without faith would certainly be empty. Everyone would be a pessimist, as optimism is based largely on faith. No one would believe that they matter in the greater scheme of life, and for many, life would be meaningless.

The truth is, we are all just minute parts of a larger picture. Our world, our universe, is so vast, but we are only exposed to a very small part of it. Although we cannot see it, we know there is more to the universe than what we have experienced. The same can be said of life—there is more to life than any of us have been given the opportunity to experience. Because of that, we can trust that, although we may not know our role in life, we are all contributing to a grander plan.

Like a pebble tossed into a pond, everything we do has a ripple effect. We do something that affects someone else, and, in turn, the effect of our deed on that person will affect the people they encounter. It could be something as small as sharing a smile. By momentarily sharing good will and brightening someone's day, we can influence their mood and outlook. In turn, they are happier and pass that happiness onto others.

Faith can be so many things, from spiritual faith to having faith in others. It could be faith that everything has a purpose and our lives are all part of a bigger plan. Or it can be the internal assurance that things will work out the way we trust them to. There is the faith of a child, faith in God, a creator, or other higher being, and faith in the unknown, oftentimes referred to as blind faith.

Spiritual or Religious Faith

Religious faith refers to the belief in God or another being. It often implies being involved in a religion and attending a church or place of worship. For some, it means attending services on a regular basis. Others may practice their faith during meal or evening prayers. Still others might believe in a God, creator, or higher being, but don't choose to be active in a particular church or religion.

Religion often provides people with doctrines or teachings to live by. The faith of its members provides them with the comfort and trust that there is a God and a life beyond death. The teachings serve as guideposts throughout their life and provide them with the reassurance that God is at their side and will welcome them into heaven.

Some people are more spiritual than religious. They believe in God or a higher being but do not practice a formal religion or attend a place of worship. However, they do have faith in a God, eternal life, or other spiritual principle. Moreover, they believe that there is something greater than they are and a world beyond the one that they can readily see.

Like I said, I also believe in something greater than me—a world which I cannot see or experience, but I have faith in its existence. This faith provides me with the assurance that I have a purpose and that there is a greater plan. For others, like Pauline Jacobi, faith has not only been a major part of their lives, but it has also saved their life.

Pauline Jacobi, 92 years old, had been shopping at Wal-Mart. After placing her groceries in her car, a young man jumped into the passenger seat, telling her he had a gun and would shoot her if she didn't give him all of her money. Rather than obliging, Jacobi told him no, saying she wasn't loaded with money. In fact, she told him no three times before turning to her faith.

Pauline Jacobi was a religious woman who read the Bible every day. She told the would-be robber that as quick as he killed her, she would go to heaven, and he would go to hell. Then she ministered her faith, asserting that Jesus was in the car with her—he goes everywhere she goes. She told him to ask God for forgiveness. She stated that tears welled in the young man's eyes as he told her he was going to go home and pray that night. Noticing that the man was openly crying, Jacobi gave him $10, which was all the money she had. He thanked her and even stopped to give her a kiss on the cheek.

Ms. Jacobi credits the power of her faith for saving her life and, hopefully, saving the young man from a life of crime. It was because of her faith that she was able to remain calm. It also compelled her to pass her faith and belief onto him.

Faith in Others

Another aspect of faith is having faith in others. I choose to believe that most people will do the right thing, live up to their word, and be responsible. Reassurance comes from knowing I can count on others when I need them and even when I don't.

Life would be full of suspicion and doubt if we didn't have faith in each other. We need to have faith in our neighbors, our employers and employees, our family and friends. We need to have faith in our doctors and caregivers. It's also important to have faith in spouses and partners—it is that faith that provides the trust necessary for the relationship to grow and endure over time.

Faith in others is all about trusting that others will do the right thing, even when they don't have to. What a cold world it would be if we didn't believe that all people have good intentions and act in the best interests of themselves and others. I believe that people want the best for themselves and others. I choose to believe that others are honest and trustworthy and I can count on them to say what they mean and mean what they say.

As children, we have that faith—faith that our parents will take care of us and keep us from harm, faith that our basic needs will be met, promises will be kept, and that there is goodness in everyone. This is true not just for people, but also for other living creatures.

A mother bird tends to her eggs, and when they hatch, her baby birds depend on her for their survival. As they grow bigger and stronger, the mother bird pushes them out of the nest, on the assumption that they will be able to fly. The little birds, trusting their mother, let her push them from their nest. Their faith is rewarded with the ability to fly and become independent.

Before we can have that type of faith and trust in each other, we must first have faith in ourselves. The mother bird had to have faith that she was doing the right thing for her babies; in other words, before she could trust their ability to fly, she had to have faith that she knew they were ready and, as their mother, she needed to let them try.

Faith in Outcomes

"Que sera sera, whatever will be, will be." Those famous lyrics, sung by Doris Day, represent the need to have faith that things will work out as they should. So many of us try to micromanage our lives and ourselves. We structure our day to complete certain tasks, and we strive to change our hair, clothing and sometimes even our features to alter our physical appearance. We want to be in charge of the outcome and end result, with no flexibility or room for variation.

But is it possible? Or is it just as possible that we are part of a grander plan and things will work out the way they are intended to—that we will turn out the way we are intended to? Rather than experiencing stress and anxiety as we feverishly seek a specific outcome, we should let go and believe, having faith that the right outcome will appear and make itself known to us. It's all part of knowing that we are where we are supposed to be, right now at this moment in time. It's trusting in a grand design, even if we don't know what that looks like at this point in time.

Faith in Ourselves

Oh, what a rough life we create when we don't have faith or belief in ourselves! We doubt that we are on the right path, whether we have the skills, talents, or abilities to accomplish our goals, and walk through life with low self-esteem when we don't have unshakeable faith and belief in ourselves. Without faith in ourselves, we stay in the shadows, unwilling to take risks. Thus, we fail to enjoy the rewards that come from being fully involved in life and the pursuit of what makes each of us happy.

A lack of faith in ourselves instills fear and doubt that causes us to miss opportunities. If we are afraid of being heartbroken, we will never experience the joy of knowing love. If we are critical of ourselves, we will hide our talents and beauty from the rest of the world and never experience the success that can come from our individuality.

We need faith in ourselves to pursue our goals and dreams; otherwise, we'd be stuck right where we are forever. A deep faith in ourselves is the support system that picks us up when we're down and protects us from criticism and negativity. Faith in ourselves is the unseen force that gives us the strength, courage, and perseverance to take a chance and overcome obstacles.

Ways to Build or Increase Faith in Yourself

1. Make a list of your talents and skills. Everybody has talents and skills, some of which are unique only to them. Create a list of all of the things you can do, are good at, or unusual talents you may have. If you don't know your talents and skills, ask your friends and family or write down the things that you are complimented on most frequently.

2. Make goals. Better yet, take steps to achieve them. With each accomplishment or milestone reached, you'll increase your confidence and the faith that you can do anything you set your mind to.

3.   Give yourself permission to fail. No one excels at everything they attempt the first time. We fell when we took our first steps and toppled our bikes a time or two. Sometimes it takes a few times before we can master what we set out to do. Don't give up if you fail—learn what you did wrong and use it to improve the next time.

4.   Forgive yourself. Did you make a mistake? It's not the end of the world. Everyone makes mistakes, and everyone has the opportunity to grow from their mistakes. Don't dwell on the past; instead, look forward to the future.

5.   Give yourself a break. When you're feeling particularly challenged, take a break. Step back and rest. Rebuild your determination and your desire to accomplish your goals. By not quitting, you'll build faith in yourself and believe in your ability to succeed.

6.   Surround yourself with people who believe in you. If believing in yourself is a struggle, then expose yourself to people who do. The unconditional love of a parent, child, or even a pet will remind you that you have good qualities and characteristics to contribute to the world.

7.   If you want to believe in yourself, believe in something else. Find a cause, a hobby, or something that is important to you and get involved with it. Join an organization, volunteer, make others aware ... whatever it is, when you believe in something passionately and become actively involved in it, you can't help but increase the faith and belief you have in yourself.

Benefits of Having Faith

1.   People who have faith in their lives are happier.

2.   Faith decreases stress and anxiety.

3.   Faith increases our endurance and perseverance, making us more likely to achieve our goals.

4.   Faith gives us the confidence to try new things and make changes in life.

5.   Faith instills our life with peace and a sense of purpose.

6.   Faith increases positivity and reduces negativity.

7.   People who have faith in God or a higher being are healthier and may live longer than those who don't.

Approximately 600 seriously ill hospital patients participated in a study conducted by Duke University Medical Centre and Bowling Green State University.

Approximately 95% of them considered themselves to be religious. When facing their illness, those who blamed God or lacked faith were nearly 28% more likely to die than those who had faith—in God, in themselves, and in a positive outcome.

Have faith in yourself. Have faith in others. Have faith in a greater power or being and live your life knowing that things will work out as they are intended to. These are all examples of faith—something that's invisible, yet so powerful. Faith has been said to move mountains; at the very least, it gives us the strength to climb and conquer mountains. This lesson has been instilled in us since we were children, since the days of reading *The Little Engine that Could.* If the little train in that story hadn't repeatedly told himself, "I think I can, I think I can, I think I can!" the little train wouldn't have tried. He would have never known his capabilities or whether he could make it up the mountain. In this example, we can certainly see that while faith may not actually be able to move mountains, it is powerful enough to move us up the mountain. And once we're there, we're on top of the world, knowing that's just where we are supposed to be at this moment in time.

"When we stop micromanaging our lives,
we can allow many wonderful things to happen."
- Shelly Cady

Chapter Six

Everything Happens for a Purpose: Find the Lesson

"The purpose of life is a life of purpose."
— Robert Bryne

CHOOSING TO SEE THE bright side is an attitude that I've chosen to adopt. To me, life is always good, even when it isn't. Confused? Let me explain.

At an early age, I learned that my life would be what I made it. My father worked and was gone a great deal of the time, and my mother, while she was home, was emotionally unavailable. As a young girl, I'd come home from school to find my mom in bed. I quickly learned that if I was going to eat, it was up to me to pour myself a bowl of cereal or make a sandwich. When I finished and had nothing to do, I'd play by myself. This pattern continued for many years. I wasn't angry with my parents; I just understood that my life was what it was. These were my circumstances, and it was up to me to make the best of them.

I carry that principle with me today. Life isn't always a bowl of cherries and everything doesn't come up roses all of the time. It can't. There are just far too many things that we cannot control. I've learned that even when "bad" things happen, and they will, the impact they have on my life will be the direct result of how I react, not the fact that they happened.

I've never been a woe-is-me kind of person. We all have events or stages in life that are high or low. And I believe there is a reason. Everything in life has a purpose—we cannot appreciate happiness without experiencing sadness. We cannot experience growth without learning from setbacks. We cannot progress without learning how to overcome challenges and obstacles. For everything that happens in our lives, there is a lesson to be learned. In other words, everything that happens in our life, good or bad, has a purpose.

I don't believe in chance. Life isn't a series of coincidences or a scramble against odds. Things happen for a reason. People come into our life for a reason. Our jobs, finances, health, and relationships change for a reason. The following story of how two strangers met is a perfect example.

Emily Nappi and Mikayla Stern-Ellis were both raised in California. Both girls chose the same college, Tulane University in New Orleans. As freshmen, they met online during the dorm roommate process. While they didn't become roommates, they did keep in touch, usually through Facebook. A friendship formed as they discovered they both love acting and have the same taste in clothes. Friends even pointed out how much they resembled each other. It was a Facebook post by Mikayla, commenting about her Colombian sperm donor (her biological father), that changed their relationship. Emily read Mikayla's status update and was shocked because she, too, was conceived using a sperm donor, who was also from Colombia. After checking the identification number of the sperm donor who was their biological father, the two girls learned that they were half sisters.

Is this a series of mind-boggling coincidences? I don't think so. Instead, I like to think it was part of a grand design. They were supposed to meet, and I believe there is a purpose, whether it is for family, love, health, or another reason yet to be learned. They were compelled to attend the same college, so far from their homes, for a reason.

How do such events, such life occurrences, allow us to open our perspective? When the event is heartwarming, it helps us to see that there is more to life than we can see from our perspective. But even more significant are those events and life occurrences that aren't so heart touching. I believe when life hands us lemons that it's not because we have rotten luck or we are in the wrong place at the wrong time. The real reason we encounter trying times is so we can learn something from the experience. It's an opportunity for us to correct our path or focus on what is most important.

Unfortunately, though, when misfortune strikes, most people focus only on what happened and the fact that they wish it hadn't. They let it bring them down, and sometimes keep them there. They dwell on their bad luck, bad timing, and even let it prevent them from moving forward. Negative thoughts are infused into these situations, and ultimately, they instill self-doubt and a lack of confidence or faith that the situation or obstacle can be conquered and overcome.

For example, let's say a person applied for what was their "dream job." Instead of ascertaining why or improving their qualifications, resume, or interview skills, they accept that they are not qualified or suitable and never try again. A person who is diagnosed with a serious illness or has an injury or disability can yell at the gods and feel self-pity, while accepting their limitations, instead of enjoying the life they do have today, at this very minute, and putting extra effort into overcoming their challenges.

It's all in the mindset that we create for ourselves. Washington Irving once said, "Great minds have purpose, others have wishes. Little minds are tamed and subdued by misfortunes; but great minds rise above them." When we choose to look at life occurrences and events as more than inconveniences or setbacks, we open ourselves up to possibilities. How?

First, we have to understand that there is a purpose for what has happened. It was supposed to happen, and we are supposed to learn something from it. Even if we cannot see it at the time, there is a plan and a lesson that we can take from every situation or event ... and we can use it to become stronger, wiser, and better.

So often, I have not paid attention to an event that occurred, much less the lesson. Then what happened? It occurred again! Oh, maybe it was not the same exact incident, but another that bears a quite similar lesson—the same lesson that I did not learn the first time around. It's proof to me that when we miss an opportunity to learn and grow, the opportunity will continue to present itself, often in unpopular ways. Each time, that lesson becomes a little stronger. The first time, it might be like a whisper, very subtle. The next time, it's more apparent and makes itself known. The more often we ignore or miss the lesson, the louder and louder it becomes, until it finally screams at us to recognize it.

I don't wish for misfortune; however, I do find that setbacks can be gifts in disguise. Everything that occurs in our life has a purpose and a lesson. Everything that happens allows us the opportunity to grow and learn. How amazing is that?! When an event occurs in our life that may not be what we were expecting, or that we were wanting, we need to take a step back and look at it. We need to decipher what we can take from it or what we are supposed to learn from it. Try and look at it through the eyes of another person, an observer, rather than being directly involved and emotionally attached to it. Ask yourself, what can I gain from this event? How can I use it to avoid repeating it again? In what way can I apply what I've learned here to grow and improve my life in the future?

Take it one step further and ask yourself what you would have gained if the event had worked out the way you wanted it to. Now, look at the different lesson you gained instead. Can you see a benefit to this lesson and how it might make you stronger than if everything had panned out precisely like you wanted it to? If not, take another look ... the lesson is there; it's waiting for you to grasp it.

Of course, there are events for which we might not have answers. We might not be able to understand the why. Sometimes, there can be no conceivable explanation when something happens. As a result, it can be difficult, if not impossible, to determine the lesson. In that case, we can only trust that the answers will come in time. We also should consider the fact that it might not be a lesson, per se, that we are being exposed to. Maybe we're being exposed to new perspectives and viewpoints. Maybe we're supposed to grow and become stronger as a result. Those are things that we can focus on even if we don't comprehend the underlying lesson.

Here's an example. "Joe" is a successful executive—he's a power guy, someone who drives himself harder than he drives anyone else. A stereotypical Type A personality and workaholic, Joe is the first one at the office and the last one to leave. He's very good at what he does. Just 50 years old, the world is his oyster and the future holds much promise and success for him.

Joe wakes up one Monday morning with chest pains. Rushed to the emergency room, he's treated for a heart attack and wheeled into surgery. Joe's relatively young to have such significant health problems, and he's not familiar with "down time." It's inconvenient, and he has too much to do! But as he accepts that there is nothing he can do to change it, Joe finds the lesson, the gift, in his misfortune. The lesson is that he needs to slow down and take better care of himself—the gift is the love and concern he sees in the eyes of his wife and children. Suddenly, Joe realizes what is truly important in life—it's not working harder and faster, but rather spending time with the people he loves.

Joe is not alone. It often takes an unexpected event to make us realize the things that are most important to us in life. While we might not welcome the event, we can certainly see that it brings us a gift—the opportunity to correct our path and appreciate what we have and the people we love.

Knowing that everything serves a purpose allows me to look for the gift, the lesson, that I know lies within it. The lesson is the gift. Life gave us an opportunity and along with it, we also received a gift, a lesson, an opportunity to grow and experience something new. It may not be what we planned or what we expected, but if we give it a chance, we might just find that the gift we received is as good as, if not better, than what we wanted.

With each lesson, we are intended to grow. We are not born with wisdom; it comes from experience. We are not given a guidebook, telling us the path to follow and stay on, when we are born. Sometimes, we go off course—and sometimes we have to be reminded of our purpose and values so we can get back on track. Regardless, with each lesson comes some growth that will help us on the rest of this journey. Even though we might not like it, the biggest growth comes from the hardest situations, the hardest and most painful lessons. Yes, sometimes lessons are painful. Sometimes, that is what is needed to make sure we don't miss the lesson and learn from it. We must experience it, and we must experience the pain that accompanies it.

"What doesn't kill you makes you stronger" is a popular saying that is quite true. Life is all about growth; if we are not growing, we are not living. Every event, situation, or person that comes into our life is there for a reason—to help us grow in some way. Sometimes, it does teach us right from wrong or help us correct mistakes. For instance, financial lessons might teach us to budget and stop making impulse purchases. Other times, the lessons are broader, but even more important. They include lessons that teach understanding, compassion, empathy, or concern. A quote by George Washington Carver represents this philosophy well.

"How far you go in life depends on your being tender with the young, compassionate with the aged, sympathetic with the striving and tolerant of the weak and strong. Because someday in your life you will have been all of these."
- George Washington Carver

Yes, even the strong are sometimes weak. The rich are sometimes poor. Life is a journey, and we need to experience many perspectives and viewpoints in order to experience life fully and grow as much as possible.

How to Learn from Mistakes

Mistakes are life events that often produce valuable lessons that we can apply to our future success and growth. When you make a mistake, rather than dwelling on what went wrong, learn from it and use the lesson in a positive way in the future. The following suggestions will help you.

- **Don't dwell on the mistake.** What's done is done. You can't go back in time and change it now. But you can learn from it so you don't repeat the same mistake in the future. Find the nugget of wisdom and take it with you, leaving the past in the past.

- **Be open to new perspectives.** Let others help you. Listen to their advice. Turn to them for support. They might not have all of the answers, but maybe the lesson you are supposed to learn is that you need people who care about you in your life. It's also true that we need support, friendship, and love the most when we are going through difficult times.

- **Forgive yourself.** Truly forgive yourself. If a particular situation is your fault and you've caused yourself or others pain, consider it a life lesson, not a life sentence. Then get studying the lesson you've just learned and apply it as you move forward.

- **Don't be angry.** Anger will affect your ability to learn the purpose behind what happened and the lesson it contains. Emotions often get in the way of our ability to see what is being presented in a rational manner. With each lesson life presents to us, we develop our judgment. Anger only clouds our judgment as it only allows us to blame ourselves, other people, or circumstances for what has occurred. When we assign blame to other people or things, we prevent ourselves from taking responsibility for either the mistake or the lesson we are meant to learn and grow from.

It is the lesson, not the circumstance or occurrence, that will have the greatest impact on our lives. Each event or occurrence serves to bring us closer to the person we are evolving to become—the person we are meant to be and can be. That's the growth that we should all seek, and it's more powerful than any misfortune or setback we'll ever encounter.

"In spite of where we were, how we had gotten here and why we had come, I felt that at this moment of our lives, this place was exactly where we belonged. We were not drifting but rising, rising toward something right and of significance."
— Dean Koontz

Chapter Seven

Be Happy!

"Happy is entirely up to you and always has been."
— Janette Rallison, *My Fair Godmother*

I CHOOSE TO BE happy every day, all day. Not sometimes. Not just when things are going well or there is something exciting to look forward to. I choose to be happy *all of the time.* I don't have to wait for a special occasion to celebrate life. Life is a gift that's far too short to waste by being sad, angry, or hurt. It's certainly too short to spend one minute of it being nonchalant, unconcerned, or indifferent. To me, that would be like taking the life out of living!

Do things happen to me that make me unhappy? Well, sure they do, just like they do to you. I'm not exempt from having problems or experiencing things that make me feel sad. But I don't let it drag me down for long. I make it a point to put myself back into that happy mode. Why? Why does it matter? So what if I am always happy? Well, first of all: Being happy just feels good! It brings me energy that makes me want to be an active participant in life and the things that are occurring around me. Who doesn't like to feel good and energetic?

The mood you are in will affect how you feel. Try it now: put a frown on your face. How do you feel? Tired? Unhappy? Negative? (You probably look the same way, too.) Now plaster a big smile on your face. Things just feel and look different! It transforms your face and your outlook. Amazingly, when you lift the corners of your mouth, you also lift your spirits. And it will also lift the spirits of those you come into contact with.

When you are always happy, people want to be around you. It feels good to be around happy, positive people. Happiness is contagious! When you are happy, you look at things differently; your perception changes. Everything around you is affected. We adapt to our environment and the tone set by others. The next time you walk into a room, pay attention to what happens. If everyone is laughing and having a good time, you'll probably smile and have a good time, too. On the contrary, if everyone is subdued and sad, your demeanor will automatically adjust and you're likely to become somber. If you have the power to influence other people to that degree, choose to infuse their life with happy emotions, rather than sad or angry ones.

We have so much power over our lives that we neglect to use. Life is all about choices and attitudes. We get to choose whether we will allow someone to bring us down or make us feel bad. We also get to choose whether we want to spend our day bursting with joy, kindness, and enthusiasm! We get to choose the attitude we interject into everything we do and we share with everyone we meet.

That choice begins the moment we wake up. We get to choose whether we want to moan and crawl back under the covers or whether we want to hop out of bed, happy that we get to experience another glorious day! Happiness is a state of mind that makes me wake up smiling every day. I don't even stop and think about it when I get out of bed. My feet hit the ground, and I just know that I am happy; there is no decision to make. It's an attitude that has become a part of who I am.

Look around. Who else around you is happy? Who is not happy? Who has reason to be happy? Who has reason to not be happy? You don't have to know the person to know if they are happy; you don't even have to talk to them. Happiness shows. It cannot be hidden. Believe me, among all the people you see, there will be many who are happy, though they have reasons to be otherwise. Hundreds of thousands of people are experiencing situations that could make them sad, worried, or upset; yet, they still find a reason to be happy.

That's because they've discovered a secret — happiness is not about what you have. It's not about having a so-called perfect life. Happiness is an attitude—a state of mind that accepts that everything isn't always the way we want it to be, but that's okay. Life isn't perfect, but we can choose to look past its imperfections.

We can choose to focus on the negative or the positive things in our life. What one person perceives to be bad can be good in another person's eyes, and vice versa. The following story depicts that statement quite well.

A wealthy man wanted to teach his young son a lesson and expose him to a life much different than his own. He took him out to the country to show him how poor people live. It was a trip that he hoped would open his son's eyes and make him appreciate everything he had.

They toured the country, looking at small rundown homes out in the middle of nowhere. There were no stores, no restaurants, and no recreational facilities to be found. They spent a couple days on a farm, where a poor family lived. On their way home, the father asked his son if he realized how poor people lived. The son said, yes, he had, indeed noticed.

"We have one dog, but they have three dogs and four chickens. We have a garden, but they have big fields. We have a swimming pool, but they have a long river that never ends. We have outside lights, but they have stars that shine brightly every night. We only have a small piece of land, compared to the land that stretches around them as far as you can see. Dad, we buy all of our food at stores and restaurants, but they grow their food and pick it fresh every day. And, Dad, we have fences and alarms to protect us, but they have friends who protect and help them."

Then, the boy shocked his father when he said, "Thank you for showing me just how poor we are, Dad."

When life gives you lemons, make lemonade is all about looking at the bright side, seeing things the way we choose to see them. No matter what our lot in life might presently be, we all have the opportunity to be happy, regardless of our circumstances.

Years ago, I read a story about an elderly woman whose choice to be happy was profound and inspirational. The story has been retold many times in various ways; however, the original author is not known. This woman was 90 years old and lived alone. Her husband had recently passed away, and it had become difficult for her to live by herself. Needing assistance, the time had come where it was necessary for her to move into a nursing home.

As always, on the morning that she was to leave the only home she'd known for the last 50-plus years, she dressed early in her freshly pressed clothes and pulled her hair back into a neat bun. When she arrived at the nursing home, she waited patiently for her room to be prepared. When the nurse came to get her, she followed with the aid of her walker. Once in the elevator, the nurse described her room, hoping to give her a visual description that would prepare her and compensate for her poor vision. She told her the walls were a soft yellow and the white curtains had delicate eyelet trim. She described the small table and chair that sat by the window and the dresser where they would put her clothes.

"I just love it!" the woman said enthusiastically.

"You haven't seen the room yet," the nurse replied. "Just wait until we get there and then let me know what you think of it."

The woman responded. "Whether I've seen the room or not has nothing to do with it. Happiness is something I can decide on ahead of time. Whether I like my new room has nothing to do with the way the furniture is arranged; it has to do with how I choose to arrange my mind. You see, I can spend all day moaning and complaining about how my body doesn't work like it used to, or I can be happy for the parts that do work. I cannot control what happens, but I can choose how I respond to it. I choose to be happy."

This woman had lost her husband and was leaving her home. She'd had vision loss and the loss of mobility and independence. Yet, she found a reason and a way to be happy, which I find very admirable.

It's all about the perspective we choose. We chose to be happy or not, in whatever situation or environment we are in. There are people who don't know where their next meal is coming from, where they are sleeping tonight, and who have health or other issues that we take for granted every day. Yet, they are happy. They are happy to be alive. They are grateful for what they do have. They have faith. They believe. They have a happy perspective and outlook on life. Happiness is so small, yet so huge! Everyone deserves to be happy, and there is no reason not to be. The tips below will help you become the happy you that you want and deserve to be!

1. Choose to be happy.

    Happiness is a choice—you get to decide if you're happy ... or not. Choose to be happy and make a conscious effort to expose yourself to things that will make you happy.

2. Smile.

    Smile and the whole world smiles with you. Well, maybe not the whole world, but a smile is contagious. When you smile even when you're not happy, you'll "catch" some happiness, while you're spreading it to others.

3. Expose yourself to happy people.

    It's not easy to be happy when you're around people who are sulking and sullen. Don't let others bring you down! Instead, spend time with people who are happy and who you truly enjoy.

4.   Engage in activities that make you happy.

What makes you happy? Maybe you enjoy feeling a warm breeze and the sun on your shoulders, swimming in the ocean, hiking up a mountain, running, spending time with children or animals, painting, cooking, or reading a good book. If you want to be happy more often, spend more time doing things that you know will make you happy.

5.   Listen to upbeat music.

Fun songs that get you grooving to the beat will lift your spirits. Music is mood altering and has the power to change your emotions. By choosing happy, upbeat music, you'll feel upbeat and energetic.

6.   Be grateful.

Find something every day to be grateful for and express your gratitude for it. Gratitude attracts even more of what makes you happy, while it stops you from focusing on lack or regret.

7.   Forgive.

Holding grudges is one of the biggest happiness killers we'll ever know. The anger that takes up residence in our minds hurts us more than the person we are upset with. Letting go of that anger and forgiving others for wrongs done will free you from being imprisoned in unhappiness. That's because when you hold a grudge, the person who is hurt the most is you.

8. Relax and clear your mind.

Stress and anxiety will impede your ability to be happy. If you are feeling stressed or worried, relax and take a few deep cleansing breaths to clear your mind. Yoga and meditation also work wonders!

Happiness is a goal that is attainable for everyone. It's available to the rich and the poor, the sick and the healthy, the strong and the weak, the young and the old. The benefits are many: happiness has been proven to make people healthier—studies have shown that people who are happy live longer than those who are not; it makes us more pleasant to be around; it attracts other happy people; happy people look younger and have more energy; happy people also have more opportunities because they don't have tunnel vision, which remains focused on what they wish was different in their lives. Therefore, they are able to see a broader perspective. Happy people are more likely to take chances—they aren't scared of the potential consequences because they are optimistic that everything will work out in the end.

Remember, in every life, rain will fall. Rather than being upset about the rain, be happy for the chance that its end will bring a bright and beautiful rainbow. In the meantime, make your heart happy and do a little dance in the rain!

"No matter where life takes me, you'll find me with a smile. Presumed to be happy, always laughing like a child. I never thought life could be this sweet! It's got me cheesing from cheek to cheek!"
— Mac Miller

Chapter Eight

Life is the Journey, Not the Destination

"The journey is what brings us happiness,
not the destination."
— Dan Millman

WHEN I WAS DRIFTING through life, I was always in a
hurry to get to that magical destination. While I never
really knew the actual destination, I knew it was
somewhere I really wanted to be — a place where I'd be
when all of my dreams and wishes came true. I lived
for that place. If you had asked me then, I couldn't
have told you where I was going, but I knew I was
going someplace, and I was in a hurry to get there. It
was as if I was on the speedway of life; maybe the
Autobahn! I worked long hours. I worked every day. I
worked hard. I rarely ever played or took time off. I got
promotions. I built businesses. I made money. I did all
of these things to get me to my ultimate destination
faster. My friends and peers admired me and my
successes. But it wasn't enough. I was missing
something, and something took the joy of out of my

everyday life. True happiness was placed on the backburner, only to be found when I reached that destination.

Then I learned what was missing. I never saw the scenery and enjoyed the moment. I never experienced life—I thought those experiences could wait until I "arrived" at my destination. I was in such a hurry to get to the place that I didn't even know, that I never saw or appreciated what I had accomplished, experienced, learned, lived, or passed by. Five, ten, fifteen years passed. Where did the time go? I began to wonder what I had accomplished. I asked myself why I had not yet reached my destination. I noticed I was no closer to that unknown destination—that place and time when everything in world would be perfect—than I was when I set out on my journey years before. Then it occurred to me that I didn't even know what that destination was—where was it that I wanted to be so badly before I allowed myself to experience and enjoy this thing called life?

I'm reminded of a poem entitled "Welcome to Holland" and written by Emily Perl Kingsley. The poem describes an expecting mother's anticipation to reach her destination—Italy. But in the end, the mother landed in Holland.

Kingsley's words reflect on the excitement of going to Italy and seeing the beautiful sights and sounds. She bought books about Italy, learned the language, and her life plans revolved around being there. But, alas, she never made it. Instead, she found herself in Holland, a place far different than her beloved Italy.

In the poem, though, Kingsley realizes that, while it certainly isn't Italy, Holland has its own beauty—it has tulips, windmills, and Rembrandts that, although much different than the Coliseum and Venice, are actually quite lovely.

Oh, what a shame it would be if we failed to see the joy and beauty of where we are each day because we wanted to be somewhere else! Kingsley's poem was actually an explanation of how it felt to anticipate having a healthy baby versus the reality of having a child with special needs, but its message relates to so much more—its message relates to this wonderful, glorious thing we call life.

We all have a dream, and, hopefully, most of us have goals. Those things are fantastic ways to help us grow and become the best we can possibly be! But should our life focus only on realizing our dreams and achieving our goals? Do we only start living once we've gotten to Italy, our dream destination?

What is your dream destination? It could be Italy. It could be retirement. It could be marriage. It might be success, fame, or fortune—or all three. Do you catch yourself putting off your life until you reach those milestones … when the kids are grown, when I retire, when I get my degree, when I'm promoted, when I have enough money, when I move to the south, north, east or west? Sure, there is nothing wrong with making plans for when those things do happen; but don't fail to sacrifice today for the dreams of tomorrow. Today has as much impact on your overall life as any other day—don't waste it because you're too busy longing for something more.

Once I stopped drifting and got in touch with my passion and purpose, I realized that there is no one destination. We are always evolving. We are always growing. We are always learning. How could I have thought that there was one final place or thing that I would achieve and then I would be "there?" I had spent all of these years in a hurry to get to a place that doesn't exist, only to realize that I was ignoring the most important thing in life: the journey. Life isn't about waiting to get to one special place, waiting for our dream job, a relationship, oodles of money, or great success to start living. I finally figured out that it's about what happens every day—the experiences, the memories, the learning, the friendships, and my family. These are the things that matter. These are the things we live for, not some future happening in life and its journey.

"The trick is to enjoy life. Don't wish away your days,
waiting for better ones ahead."
— Marjorie Pay Hinckley

We need to take time to appreciate the life we are living, as it is *right now, at this very moment*, to look at our surroundings, take pride in our accomplishments, smell the roses, appreciate and love those around us and our family and friends. We need to play and have fun—we don't have to wait until we "arrive" in Italy or another destination! We need to take time off and away from our daily life to enjoy a vacation. There is no one destination for us to race to—there are no life destinations, only geographical ones. Actually, we are already at our destination. We are already living our life.

Oh, how grand it would be if we paused to be a participant in our own lives, rather than an observer, existing through the days while we waited for something more, something better. Do you say, "I can't wait until I retire, but today I've got to go to work"? Then, you get through today and repeat the same scenario tomorrow, and every day after that ... always living for the future, not for today. How much different would your day (and your life) be if you got up every morning excited and ready to seize the day and experience everything it has to offer, saying, "Retirement will come, but today I get to go to work! I get to have fun! I get to experience new things! There is nowhere else I'd rather be!"

"Begin at once to live and count each separate day as a separate life."
~Seneca

The past is gone. The future is uncertain, but we do have today—we have this moment in time to make an impact on our own lives. If today was all you had, what would you do with it? If you're like me, you'd stop and take notice of all the things you take for granted—the sunrise and sunset, fresh air, the uniqueness of a flower petal, a child's laughter, a friend's smile, a hug from a loved one. Isn't that our destination—to enjoy life? Isn't every day our destination—it's where we are supposed to be at this moment in time? Enjoy it. It's an important part of your journey, and you never know where it can take you if you only let it.

We only have one life and our own personal journey to experience and make the most of, and we never know how long that may last, or when it may end. We get to plan that trip. We get to map out where we want to go and how we want to travel. But oh how much would we miss if we slept through it and didn't partake in the journey.

And what if we found that the "destination" wasn't all we thought it would be? What if we spent our entire life striving for something more, somewhere different, only to find when we got there, that it wasn't all it was cracked up to be? Oh, the regret we would feel for everything we missed, all we sacrificed, for this one thing … this one place, when in actuality, we already had everything we wanted and needed all along!

Perhaps the abundance we are seeking—the time, the wealth, the fame, the success, the destination—is all in the now. Every day offers an opportunity for the abundance that we all secretly and anxiously await at some point in time, until something happens that signals our "arrival." That's because the abundance we are seeking, whatever and wherever it is, isn't things, people, or places. No, it's the emotions that we anticipate we will get from those things, people, places, or period in time. Aren't those emotions already available to us, if only we paused and gave ourselves permission to notice them? Doesn't every day present an opportunity for us to laugh, to feel love, to know the satisfaction of helping others, to reward ourselves for a good deed or a job well done, to spread and receive joy so abundantly that it overflows? Those opportunities are present every day, not at some fictitious or projected future moment in time.

How full and rich our entire lives would be if we enjoyed the journey, rather than waiting until we arrive at our destination! We have an entire world to enjoy, explore, and travel. There's no reason to wait or to spend our time chasing dreams when we could be creating them instead. The problem with chasing dreams is you're always looking ahead, and the dream is always just beyond your reach and your grasp. But when you create dreams, they're right here in front of you, ready for you to enjoy them immediately.

Ric Elias happened to have a front-row seat on the infamous Flight 1549 that landed in the Hudson River. The experience changed him forever, as it would most of us. In a speech, Mr. Elias shared his touching story.

The plane was struggling, and the pilot turned off the engines and said, "Brace for impact." From that moment until the moment of impact, Ric Elias learned three things about himself.

"I learned it all changes in an instant."

As Elias states, we all have a bucket list of experiences we want to have, but we don't get to. The first thought that ran through his mind was that he wished he hadn't postponed the things he'd wanted to do. There were fences he wanted to mend and people he wanted to reach out to, and a sense of urgency and purpose overtook him.

"I regretted the time I'd wasted with things that did not matter and took away from the people that mattered."

Elias recanted the times that he'd spent on unimportant things, and in this moment, he reflected on the relationships in his life. As a result, he no longer chooses to be right, instead, he chooses to be happy.

"I only wish one thing:
I wish to see my kids grow up."

As he faced the potential end of his life, everything he'd ever wished for changed. All of the goals and dreams that he'd wanted vanished in an instant, exchanged for the one thing that he realized was more important than anything else—being with his family.

As Elias said, he was able to see into the future. If you could do so, would you change? Would your relationships change? Would your goals change? Would the things that you thought mattered change? You don't have to be facing the end of your life on the Hudson River to make those changes. Don't wait until tomorrow. Do it today. Do it right now. Start living the life you want to live. Live and love every minute and step of your journey.

Because, sometimes, what happens on your journey will change your destination. And in the end, you'll find that you're right where you've always wanted to be. It is in that place where you will find happiness. Happiness isn't a destination—it's already there. If you want to be happy, look inside of yourself and you will find the heartbeat to happiness.

About Shelly Cady

SHELLY IS A SPEAKER, trainer, and the author of *Heartbeat to Happiness: Eight Principles of Living a Happy Life*. She is also the creator of the "Heartbeat to Happiness" training program.

Shelly has been a successful sales professional, manager, leader, business owner and entrepreneur for over 30 years. She has a diversified professional background that has enhanced her life experiences so that she offers her audience and clients a message and training that all can relate to.

Through her strong background in sales and management in Corporate America and her successful journey as a business owner and entrepreneur, she has developed a strong understanding of the challenges that people today experience, as well as the value in personal and professional development and how it directly influences ones performance in their personal and professional lives.

Shelly is passionate about helping business owners, entrepreneurs, professionals, and others willing to learn, that through effective teamwork and shifting of their perspectives, they can indeed obtain whatever their heart desires.

Shelly has received numerous leadership awards and certifications in the companies and associations in which she has been involved. She holds a Bachelors degree in Business Management from the University of Phoenix. Originally from St. Louis, Missouri, she now resides in Southern California.

www.HeartbeatToHappiness.com

www.ingramcontent.com/pod-product-compliance
Lightning Source LLC
Chambersburg PA
CBHW072239290326
41934CB00008BB/1352